Check out this dog!
His name is Sam.... Sam Superalert.
And he is no ordinary dog either... he is a superdog!

Whenever a kid is in trouble, Sam will be there in a flash!

He's got superpowers too!
I mean, what's a superdog without superpowers? Just a dog, I guess.

He has super hearing!
He could hear an ant whispering from a hundred miles away.

He has super speed!
He could beat an airplane to the end of a runway.

And, coolest of all, he has super-tech!
He's so clever, that he can invent machines
most humans could only dream of.

He once invented the 'Dog-A-Lator', A computer he wore on his chest that translated his barking into any language. It's how he speaks to humans.

He once built a 'Dog-O-Porter',
Like a teleporter, but for dogs. It will take you to any park in the world.

But his favorite creation was the 'Dog-A-Pult',
A cannon that launched him into the air so he could fly!

One day, he was showing his friend, Scotty the Scottie, his latest project, when his Dog Alert went off.

"Now as you can see," he began, pointing at his blueprints, "the 'Dog-Mobile' is going to be unlike any superhero car you have ever seen."

"Excuse me a moment," he said to Scotty.
"Someone's in trouble."
"That's quite alright," said Scotty.
Sam bounded over to the window, opened it up,
and stretched his ear into the air. This is what
he heard...

"But I'm hungry,"said a boy's voice.
    "So am I. Give me your lunch money," said a second.
    "But..." the first boy began.
    "Give it to me or you'll be sorry," warned the second.

"Oh dear,"said Sam.

"What is it?" asked Scotty.

"A severe case of bullying," said Sam. "Over at Flagstone Elementary on 49 th Street. I have to go?"

"How do you know where to go?" asked Scotty.

"I'm super! That's how," said Sam with a wink. "Fetch ya later."

And with that, Sam leaped into the 'Dog-O-Porter', pulled the lever and vanished with a 'POP'!

Sam reappeared in the park just across the road from the school. He sprinted over the road and poked his head through the bushes.

On the other side was a playground. He didn't like what he saw...

A huge blond boy was holding a small dark-haired boy
against a wall, where nobody else could see.
"Fine," said the small boy. "Here. Take it."
He handed over the coins from his pocket.
"Is that it?" the blond boy said. "Thanks anyway, dweeb."
He gave the small boy a final shove and walked off.

"Hey!" the boy shouted.

"Having a bit of bully trouble I see," said Sam.

"Um, yes. That's Barry. He's always bullying me. Who are you?" the boy asked.

"My name's Sam Superalert," said Sam. "I'm here to help. What's your name?"

"Diego," said the boy. "And I could use some help."

"I've got loads of tricks for dealing with bullies," said Sam.
"Want to come back to my doghouse?"
"Your doghouse?" questioned Diego.
"It's OK," said Sam. "It's a super doghouse. There's loads of cool tech in there. I'm a superdog, you see."
"Ummmm... OK then," agreed Diego.

When they entered the doghouse, Diego gasped. "Woah. This is the craziest doghouse I've ever seen!" he said.

"Told you it was cool," said Sam. "Now, shall we begin your anti-bully training?"

"Yes, please," replied Diego.

"OK. So, lesson one is all about body language. You need to puff out your chest to show you aren't scared of him."

"Try it on my dog-bot here," Sam continued. A robot, with the body of a man, but the head of a poodle, walked over.

"I'll set him to 'Intimidation Training Mode'," said Sam.

So, Diego puffed out his chest, as Sam had taught him. He did his best to look completely confident. After a few tries, the dog-bot ran away screaming.

"Amazing!" whooped Sam. "Now for lesson two. If the bully chooses violence, like shoving or kicking, you must learn to dodge them." Sam set the dog-bot to 'Combat Training Mode'.

Diego spent the next hour learning how to avoid everything the dog-bot threw at him. By the end, he could duck every punch, swerve every shove, and jump every kick!

"Amazing!" whooped Sam. "Now for lesson three. Once you have shown you are not afraid and avoided any violence, you must walk away."

"That's easy!" said Diego.

"Not as easy as you think," said Sam.

"When we get angry or upset, it's very easy to lash out. You might want to yell at the bully or hit him back. It takes a lot of strength to do nothing."

"But if I walk away and do nothing, the bully will get away with it," said Diego.
"Not if you follow lesson four!" said Sam.
"And what's that?" asked Diego.
"Once you have walked away, you must go and tell an adult. They will always know what to do."

Sam and Diego hopped through the bush into the playground. But Sam turned to leave right away!

"Nice to meet you, Diego. And good luck," he said.

"You're not staying?" said Diego.

"I can only give you the tools," explained Sam, "but I can't solve your problem for you. You need to do this on your own."

"OK then," gulped Diego.

"I believe in you. Here he comes," said Sam, pointing at Barry, who was stomping towards them.
"How will you know what happens?" asked Diego.
I'm a superdog. That's how," Sam said.
"Fetch ya later." He winked and disappeared through the bush.

"Hey. I'm hungry. Got any more money?" yelled Barry.
"I'm not afraid of you," said Diego, puffing out his chest.
"What's happening?" said Barry, confused.
"No more taking my stuff. I've had enough!" announced Diego.
"How dare you talk to me like that," yelled Barry, clenching his fists.
"You can try but you won't hit me?" said Diego.

"Sure, I will," said Barry. "Watch!"

But try though Barry did, he didn't hit Diego once.
He ducked every punch,
Swerved every shove,
And jumped every kick!
In no time at all, Barry was completely out of breath.

"AAAARGH! How are you doing this, dweeb?"
he yelled. "You're in trouble now."
"Oh no... I think you're the one in trouble,"
said Diego, as he calmly walked off to find
a teacher.

Minutes later, Sam flicked on his TV surveillance system in his doghouse. It showed a teacher pulling Barry across the playground by the ear. She was giving him a stern talking to. Diego was following close behind looking very proud of himself.

"Well done kid," Sam said to himself.
"Knew you could do it. Another day. Another kid saved."
That's what Sam really loved.
All the gadgets... sure, they were great.
But days like this, when he got to help kids like Diego...
that's what got him out of dog bed in the morning.

Sam let out a big yawn.

"Ooof. I'm dog tired," he said. And with that, he curled up in dog bed, safe in the knowledge it had been another super day being a superdog.

Made in the USA
Middletown, DE
26 March 2023

27566098R00018